Mon Gets Wet

By Sally Cowan

Mon is on a big log.

He can see lots of figs.

"No, Mon!" said Mum.

"The log can tip!"

But Mon ran up the big log.

The big log tips!

Mon got wet!

"Get up, Mon!" said Mum.

"We can look for nuts."

Mon ran to Mum.

But he ran into a big web!

Mon tugs at the web.

Mon sobs and sobs.

Mum led Mon up a log.

I quit!
I am wet and I did not get the figs!

Mum let Mon
get lots of nuts.

CHECKING FOR MEANING

1. How does Mon fall into the water? *(Literal)*

2. Who rescues Mon from the spider's web? *(Literal)*

3. What does Mon mean when he says, *I quit!*? *(Inferential)*

EXTENDING VOCABULARY

wet	Look at the word *wet*. Find two other words in the book that rhyme with *wet*. Can you think of any other words that rhyme with *wet*?
nuts	What is the base of the word *nuts*? How has adding *s* to the base changed the meaning?
quit	The word *quit* means to give up. What could Mon have said instead of *I quit*?

MOVING BEYOND THE TEXT

1. What did Mon eat in the story? What else do monkeys eat?

2. Describe where monkeys live.

3. What have you given up on because it was too hard?

4. What advice would you give Mon about getting the figs?

SPEED SOUNDS

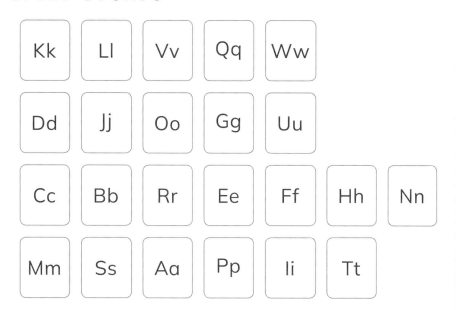

Kk	Ll	Vv	Qq	Ww		
Dd	Jj	Oo	Gg	Uu		
Cc	Bb	Rr	Ee	Ff	Hh	Nn
Mm	Ss	Aa	Pp	Ii	Tt	

PRACTICE WORDS

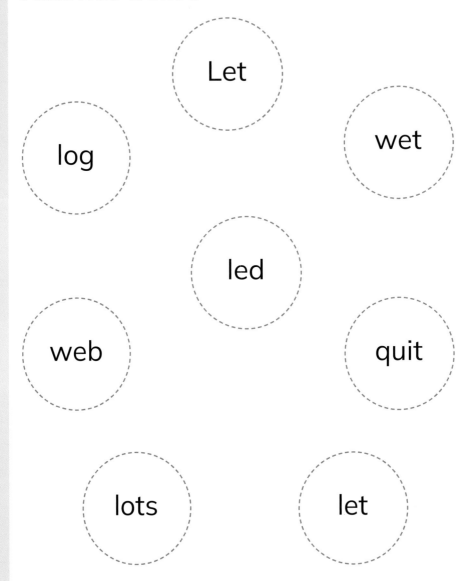

Let

wet

log

led

web

quit

lots

let